Thank You!

Bill Gothard

Psalm 1

The Secret of SUCCESS

How to Meditate

First Edition

This Book Belongs to

INSTITUTE IN BASIC YOUTH CONFLICTS

Oak Brook, Illinois 60521

Dear Alumni,

It is hard to keep a secret—especially when that secret is transforming lives and providing everything that is worth having.

When you attended your first Seminar, I enjoyed asking you, "What one activity does God guarantee will produce success in everything we do, if we faithfully carry it out?"

Those of you who attended the early Seminars heard me ask that question Tuesday evening—I could not wait until Friday to explain the principle of meditation.

I know that most of you went away from the Seminar excited about the potential of meditating on Scripture. Many of you tried to do it. Over the years I have received thrilling testimonies of what God accomplished in your lives as a result.

In recent years, God has deepened our understanding of meditation by providing new insights on how to engraft His Word into our souls. This process has been an important step in conquering destructive habits.

Many of you, however, have quietly set aside meditation with the intention that someday you will get back to it. It is for you that I am especially excited to be able to share the new insights that we have learned from this study of sheep.

With the floods of iniquity engulfing our nation, it has never been more important or urgent that God's people experience and enjoy the daily cleansing of Scripture meditation. The difference this could make in our country is beyond our comprehension.

Let's reaffirm our commitment to love the Lord Jesus Christ and to build our lives around the principles of His Word.

Through Christ our Lord,

Bill Gothard

CONTENTS

- **What are the rewards of meditating?** 4
- **Why am I not able to meditate?** 5
- **Why is accountability vital?** 5
- **Where should I begin to memorize?** 7–8
- **What will hinder meditation?** 9
- **How can I understand Scripture?** 10
- **How can I begin memorizing?** 11
- **How can Scripture be visualized?** 12
- **Why should I begin in the morning?** 13
- **Why does the shepherd anoint sheep?** 14
- **How does rumination teach meditation?** ... 15
- **What if I forget what I memorize?** 16
- **How does meditation take place?** 17
- **Why must exercise follow meditation?** 18
- **How does God encourage meditation?** 19
- **What are some results in those who have meditated?** 20

HOW DO THE EATING HABITS OF SHEEP REVEAL IMPORTANT SECRETS OF MEDITATION?

God compares Christians to sheep.

Analogies between sheep and Christians abound in Scripture. The importance of this fact cannot be overemphasized.

Those who minister to Christians are compared to shepherds: *"Feed the flock of God which is among you . . ."* (I Peter 5:2). Christ is pictured as the Chief Shepherd: *"And when the chief Shepherd shall appear . . ."* (I Peter 5:4). Christians are the sheep of God's flock: *". . . We are . . . the sheep of his pasture"* (Psalm 100:3).

Important aspects of the Christian life are also illustrated by the ways of sheep. Christians are to follow the Lord as sheep follow their shepherd. *"My sheep hear my voice, and I know them, and they follow me"* (John 10:27). Christians wander from truth the same way that sheep go astray. *"All we like sheep have gone astray . . ."* (Isaiah 53:6).

Sheep belong to the class of animals called *ruminants*, because they chew and rechew their food through a process of reingestion. Within this class, sheep are unique in many ways. The special characteristics which they possess are the very ones which the Lord used in His analogies between sheep and Christians.

As we discover these unique characteristics and apply them to our walk with the Lord, we will experience the success which God promises to those who meditate on His Word day and night.

THE RICH REWARDS OF "RUMINATING" ON GOD'S WORD

- **YOU WILL ENJOY SUCCESS.**

  "This book of the law shall not depart out of thy mouth; but thou shalt meditate therein day and night, that thou mayest observe to do according to all that is written therein: for then thou shalt make thy way prosperous, and then thou shalt have good success" (Joshua 1:8).

- **WHATEVER YOU DO WILL PROSPER.**

  "But his delight is in the law of the Lord; and in his law doth he meditate day and night. And he shall be like a tree planted by the rivers of water, that bringeth forth his fruit in his season; his leaf also shall not wither; and whatsoever he doeth shall prosper" (Psalm 1:2–3).

- **YOU WILL BE WISER THAN ALL YOUR ENEMIES.**

  "O how love I thy law! it is my meditation all the day. Thou through thy commandments hast made me wiser than mine enemies: for they are ever with me" (Psalm 119:97–98).

- **YOU WILL BE WISER THAN ALL YOUR TEACHERS.**

  "I have more understanding than all my teachers: for thy testimonies are my meditation. I understand more than the ancients, because I keep thy precepts" (Psalm 119:99–100).

- **YOU WILL BE FILLED WITH JOY.**

  "My soul shall be satisfied as with marrow and fatness; and my mouth shall praise thee with joyful lips: When I remember thee upon my bed, and meditate on thee in the night watches" (Psalm 63:5–6).

- **YOUR SUCCESS WILL BE OBVIOUS TO ALL.**

  "Meditate upon these things; give thyself wholly to them; that thy profiting may appear to all" (I Timothy 4:15).

KNOWING THAT MEDITATION IS SO REWARDING, WHY DON'T MOST CHRISTIANS MEDITATE?

Most Christians have never stopped to fully consider why God consistently compares them to sheep. It is only as a Christian understands these analogies and applies them to the preparation and process of meditation that this vital aspect of spiritual growth will become a daily experience in his Christian life.

Even before studying the following characterstics of sheep, purpose that you will apply what you learn step by step, relying upon the grace of God to do so.

"For it is God which worketh in you both to will and to do of his good pleasure" (Philippians 2:13).

1 SHEEP DO NOT HAVE THE ABILITY TO SURVIVE ON THEIR OWN.

Most people assume that sheep can take care of themselves. Nothing could be further from the truth.

Sheep are such creatures of habit that, if left to themselves, they become the victims of their own destruction. They will wander in the same paths and "graze" in the same areas until the pasture is destroyed.

Sheep will then pollute the barren ground until it breeds dangerous parasites. When thirsty, untended sheep will drink whatever water is available, even from contaminated sources such as shallow, muddy pools.

Fear, tension, and aggravation will keep sheep from properly digesting their food. Then, too, the ever-present danger of predators will bring further destruction to sheep who try to make it on their own.

No wonder Jesus made the observation of sheep that had no shepherd, *". . .They fainted, and were scattered abroad . . ." (Matthew 9:36).*

This characteristic of sheep explains why most Christians do not meditate. They assume they can do it on their own, but the clear fact of the matter is that they cannot. Their intentions may be sincere, and their motivation may be high. They may even begin a program of memorization, but in a short while they become too busy for it and soon forget about it.

If this describes your condition, there is only one remedy—accountability! In order to experience meditation on any kind of consistent basis, you must affirm the following truth and commitment:

"Having failed in my own efforts to meditate on a consistent basis, I now purpose to become accountable to another person in order to maintain this vital spiritual discipline."

Signed _____ Date _____

2 SHEEP REQUIRE A QUALIFIED SHEPHERD.

The qualities of a good shepherd are personified in the Lord Jesus Christ. He said, *"I am the good shepherd: the good shepherd giveth his life for the sheep. But he that is an hireling, and not the shepherd, whose own the sheep are not, seeth the wolf coming, and leaveth the sheep, and fleeth: and the wolf catcheth them, and scattereth the sheep. The hireling fleeth because he is an hireling, and careth not for the sheep. I am the good shepherd, and know my sheep, and am known of mine"* (John 10:11–14).

Based on this description, the one to whom you become accountable for meditation should have the following characteristics:

• He should have a personal commitment to those who are under his care.

• He should be able to persevere through times of discouragement.

• He should be able to recognize and drive away hindrances to consistent meditation.

• He must be sensitive about when to move forward on a new section and when to review what has already been engrafted.

God has ordained that pastors be His "under-shepherds" to the fathers in their congregations and that the fathers be "shepherds" to those in their own families. God has given to fathers strong protective instincts which, when properly directed, will be tremendously beneficial in helping you to become consistent in memorization and meditation.

At this point, your father may not feel that he fully qualifies; however, it would be wise for you to explain to him that you desire to be consistent in meditating on Scripture and that you would like him to keep you accountable for your goals.

Person to whom I am accountable

_____

Date we agreed _____

3 SHEEP MUST FEED IN PASTURES THAT ARE PREPARED FOR THEM.

Since the habit of sheep is to remain in the same pastures, a wise shepherd will know when to lead them to different fields and how long to keep them there.

The skillful shepherd of Psalm 23 led the sheep into green pastures. Green pastures are not common to the dry, semiarid countryside where most sheep flourish. They must be cultivated by the

shepherd, and this task requires tremendous work, time, and skill.

First, the land must be cleared of rocks, brush, roots, and stumps. It must then be plowed and seeded with special types of grain. Finally, it must be irrigated or watered.

Green fields are essential for the sheep if they are to mature properly and to produce offspring.

The one to whom you are accountable for meditation must prepare precise sections of Scripture to assign to you. These passages should relate to your present spiritual condition. If there is any hardness in your heart, the areas of resistance must be identified and appropriate portions of Scripture assigned.

If there are roots of bitterness or spiritual dryness, related Scriptures should be used to remove them.

The entire Bible is a rich green pasture in which we must feed. *". . . Man shall not live by bread alone, but by every word that proceedeth out of the mouth of God"* (Matthew 4:4). The success of meditation comes as we *". . . observe to do according to all that is written therein . . ."* (Joshua 1:8).

In another sense, however, the Bible is like a menu of different spiritual food for specific times and needs. Have the one to whom you are accountable select one of the following passages that he or she feels would be most helpful to you at this time and then fill in the date by which you should have it memorized.

BASIC SCRIPTURE PASSAGES TO BE MEMORIZED FOR MEDITATION

☐ **MATTHEW 5–7**
THE SERMON ON THE MOUNT

This is a summary of Christ's message during His earthly ministry. It is rich with foundational principles in all aspects of Christian living. Its significance was further emphasized by Paul when he said that he based sound doctrine on two things: Christ's own words and that which leads to Christ-like living. (See I Timothy 6:3.)

Date to be completed _____

Date quoted _____

☐ **ROMANS 6–8**
HOW TO HAVE VICTORY OVER SINFUL HABITS

Romans 6 explains how we are to reckon ourselves dead to sin and alive to God by entering into our victory in Christ and daily yielding the members of our bodies to God. Romans 7 describes the law of sin which operates much like the law of gravity; however, Romans 8 explains how we can live above the law of sin by the power of the Holy Spirit.

Date to be completed _____

Date quoted _____

☐ **EXODUS 20–22**
PRINCIPLES OF GOD'S LAW

The law is a schoolmaster to bring us to Christ, and the righteousness of the law is to be fulfilled in us by the Holy Spirit. This passage summarizes the law and supplies related case studies. It explains the cause-and-effect sequence of the laws of the harvest spoken of in Galatians 6:7–10.

Date to be completed _____

Date quoted _____

☐ **JAMES 1–5**
HOW TO APPLY FAITH TO PRACTICAL LIVING

Chapter 1 instructs us how to overcome temptation. Chapter 2 emphasizes the importance of putting our faith to work. Chapter 3 teaches us how to tame our tongue. Chapter 4 explains how to conquer pride and resulting contentions. Chapter 5 gives practical business principles and direction for healing.

Date to be completed _____

Date quoted _____

☐ **HEBREWS 11:1–6, 12:1–7, 13:1–8**
UNDERSTANDING PURPOSES OF CHASTENING

Chapter 11 establishes the absolute importance of faith. Chapter 12 describes the discipline required of us so that we might produce "the peaceable fruit of righteousness." Chapter 13 lists the vital relationships that Christians must maintain.

Date to be completed _____

Date quoted _____

☐ **I CORINTHIANS 13**
HOW TO DEVELOP GENUINE LOVE

This vital chapter defines the love that every Christian must develop by the grace of God. The entire Old Testament is summed up in the command to love the Lord and to love our neighbor. By engrafting this chapter and relating it to other sections of Scripture, we will learn how to fulfill the greatest commandment.

Date to be completed _____

Date quoted _____

☐ **ROMANS 12**
HOW TO DISCOVER YOUR
SPIRITUAL GIFT

Every Christian has a spiritual gift. By using it properly we experience joy, fulfillment, and fruitfulness. This chapter identifies the prerequisites for gifts and the practical use of them in ministering God's love to others.

Date to be completed _____

Date quoted _____

☐ **ROMANS 13**
HOW TO UNDERSTAND AUTHORITY

Only as we see authority figures in the perspective of this chapter will we be able to respond properly to them and to gain God's protection and direction through them. Every Christian needs to understand and to apply the essential concepts of power and influence.

Dated to be completed _____

Date quoted _____

☐ **EPHESIANS 5–6**
HOW TO BE EQUIPPED FOR WARFARE

The first chapters of Ephesians establish our position of victory in Christ. Chapter 5 identifies the works of darkness and the resulting relationships that grow out of being filled with God's Spirit. Our ability to carry out these relationships depends upon how faithful we are in putting on the whole armor of God listed in chapter 6.

Date to be completed _____

Date quoted _____

☐ **I PETER 1–5**
HOW TO SUFFER VICTORIOUSLY

By engrafting this book, we can be prepared when fiery trials overtake us. We will view them as opportunities to follow in the footsteps of Christ. The practical instruction of this book is essential for every Christian who wants to influence his or her world, since all those who live Godly lives will suffer persecution.

Date to be completed _____

Date quoted _____

☐ **GALATIANS 5:13–6:10**
HOW TO HAVE THE FRUIT OF
THE SPIRIT

The works of the flesh and the fruit of the Spirit are both defined and clarified by this passage. It also provides clear instruction on how we can demonstrate the law of love to fellow Christians.

Date to be completed _____

Date quoted _____

☐ **PSALMS 1, 15, 19, 25, 34, 37, 112, 139**
HOW TO BE ONE AFTER GOD'S
OWN HEART

God called David a man after His own heart. The more that the Psalms become ours, the more God can say the same of us. Learning the Psalms will teach Christians to pray, to sing, to rejoice, to praise, and to know the God who cares deeply about every aspect of their lives.

Date to be completed _____

Date quoted _____

☐ **PROVERBS 3**
HOW TO ENJOY THE TREASURES
OF WISDOM

Mastering the entire book of Proverbs is essential for Christians who desire to gain wise counsel for daily decisions. Every effort to memorize in this book will be greatly rewarded. Chapter 3 gives practical instruction on how to "find favor and good understanding in the sight of God and man."

Date to be completed _____

Date quoted _____

4 SHEEP MUST BE PROTECTED WHILE THEY EAT.

Sheep are defenseless. They have no way of protecting themselves. They cannot kick, bite, or hide. In fact, they cannot even run away from the enemies that prey upon them.

The normal body temperature of sheep is 103°F. If they run very long, their thick coats of wool will cause their body temperature to rise dangerously, and then they will die.

Since sheep have no built-in defense system, they have many who prey upon them. Chief among these are lions, bears, and wolves. These predators stalk the sheep day and night, placing the sheep in need of continuous protection. One of the chief functions of a shepherd is to guard the sheep.

God compares Satan to a roaring lion, seeking whom he may devour. (See I Peter 5:8.) False teachers are pictured as ravenous wolves who creep into flocks and carry away captive the young and the weak. Sometimes they enter under the guise of being sheep themselves. Jesus warned, *"Beware of false prophets, which come to you in sheep's clothing, but inwardly they are ravening wolves"* (Matthew 7:15).

SPOTTING VICIOUS ENEMIES

Cults are counterfeits of the Christian faith. They often use the Bible in their teachings, but they distort and misapply verses in an attempt to support false conclusions.

The Christian who meditates upon God's Word should be able to detect false cults quickly. However, it is also the responsibility of the shepherd to expose false teachers and to protect the flock from them.

AVOIDING POISONOUS FOODS

Lions, bears, and wolves are not the only danger from which the sheep need to be guarded. They also need protection from poisonous plants which grow among the grass they eat.

Sheep will eat any green plants they find, even if they are poisonous. Once eaten, these plants will cause severe damage or death. For this reason, the shepherd must go into a field and prepare it for the sheep by searching out, pulling up, and destroying any poisonous plants.

The same precautions are necessary to protect sheep from polluted water. On the way to pure

9

streams, sheep may stop and drink from germ-infested puddles. Here they can pick up various parasites and diseases.

This preparation is also the responsibility of the "under-shepherds" of Christ. They must identify worldly philosophies and humanistic presuppositions that so easily creep into teaching materials.

Colossians 2:8 warns that we are to let no one deceive us "... *through philosophy and vain deceit, after the tradition of men, after the rudiments of the world, and not after Christ.*"

We are also commanded in II Corinthians 10:5 to bring every thought into captivity to the obedience of Christ.

DISCERNING DOCTRINAL HERESIES

Just as sheep can eat too much of one thing, such as clover, and become bloated, so a Christian can overemphasize one truth and become heretical and schismatic. Every Biblical truth has a balancing truth: law is balanced with grace; justice is balanced with mercy; work is balanced with rest; love is balanced with truth.

Truth out of balance leads to heresy.

5 SHEEP EAT DOWN TO THE ROOTS OF THEIR FOOD.

Sheep "nip" away at the living plants until they reach the roots. For this reason they are called "nippers." Cows, on the other hand, simply tear off the top part of the grass or plants.

In preparation for meditation, Christians must also go beyond the surface thoughts and ideas of the verses. They must get down to the roots of words and phrases in order to comprehend their fuller meanings.

Learning to use a Hebrew/Greek Concordance and other references will aid a Christian greatly in accomplishing this.

For example, in the back of *Strong's Exhaustive Concordance* are Hebrew and Greek dictionaries. By looking up the word and its number in the concordance and then finding the same number in the appropriate dictionary, one can determine the root meanings of words.

CONCORDANCE

MEDITATION

consider my *m*	Ps 5:1	1901
the *m* of my heart, be acceptable	Ps 19:14	1902
the *m* of my heart shall be of	Ps 49:3	1900
My *m* of him shall be sweet	Ps 104:34	7879
it is my *m* all the day	Ps 119:97	7881
for thy testimonies are my *m*	Ps 119:99	7881

1897. הָגָה **hâgâh**, *haw-gaw'*; a prim. root [comp. 1901]; to *murmur* (in pleasure or anger); by impl. to *ponder:*—imagine, meditate, mourn, mutter, roar, × sore, speak, study, talk, utter.

1898. הָגָה **hâgâh**, *haw-gaw'*; a prim. root; to *remove:*—stay, take away.

1899. הֶגֶה **hegeh**, *heh'-geh*; from 1897; a *muttering* (in sighing, thought, or as thunder):—mourning, sound, tale.

1900. הָגוּת **hâgûwth**, *haw-gooth'*; from 1897; *musing:*—meditation.

1901. הָגִיג **hâgîyg**, *haw-gheeg'*; from an unused root akin to 1897; prop. a *murmur*, i.e. *complaint:*—meditation, musing.

1902. הִגָּיוֹן **higgâyôwn**, *hig-gaw-yone'*; intens. from 1897; a *murmuring* sound, i.e. a musical notation (prob. similar to the modern *affettuoso* to indicate solemnity of movement); by impl. a *machination:*—device, Higgaion, meditation, solemn sound.

7878. שִׂיחַ **sîyach**, *see'-akh*; a prim. root; to *ponder*, i.e. (by impl.) *converse* (with oneself, and hence aloud) or (trans.) *utter:*—commune, complain, declare, meditate, muse, pray, speak, talk (with).

7879. שִׂיחַ **sîyach**, *see'-akh*; from 7878; a *contemplation*; by impl. an *utterance:*—babbling, communication, complaint, meditation, prayer, talk.

7880. שִׂיחַ **sîyach**, *see'-akh*; from 7878; a *shoot* (as if *uttered* or put forth), i.e. (gen.) *shrubbery:*—bush, plant, shrub.

7881. שִׂיחָה **sîychâh**, *see-khaw'*; fem. of 7879; *reflection*; by extens. *devotion:*—meditation, prayer.

6 SHEEP FINISH EATING BEFORE THEY DIGEST ANY OF THEIR FOOD.

The digestive system of many animals is activated as soon as they swallow food. This is not true of sheep.

Sheep will eat and swallow a sufficient portion

of food. Most of this food collects in the first of its four stomach compartments called the *rumen* or *paunch*, which is designed to hold larger pieces of food. This compartment does not contain any digestive juices.

THE IMPORTANCE OF MEMORIZING LARGE PASSAGES OF SCRIPTURE

Just as the sheep take in large amounts of food before they digest it, so Christians should read and memorize large sections of Scripture. By doing this, we will establish an inward resource upon which to meditate, and as we meditate, we will see each verse from its larger perspective.

This practice will decrease the danger of misinterpreting a single verse or a Scriptural idea. It will also allow the Holy Spirit to reveal basic principles and their practical applications so that we can rightly divide the Word of truth. (See II Timothy 2:15.)

HOW TO MEMORIZE SO THAT YOU CAN BEGIN TO MEDITATE

Just as sheep need assistance in the feeding process, so most Christians need help in memorizing Scripture. Establish a time to meet with a friend for memorization. Try the following five-point method:

1. As your friend reads a verse to you, write down the first letter of each word you hear. Group the letters in phrases. Psalm 1:1 would look like this on your sheet:

    BITMTWNITCOTU   NSITWOS
                 NSITSOTS

2. As your friend reads the verse again, check that you have all the letters.

3. Read the verse from the Bible yourself, maintaining the inflection of the verse and picturing the meaning.
    "Blessed is the man that walketh not in the counsel of the ungodly, nor standeth in the way of sinners, nor sitteth in the seat of the scornful."

4. Repeat the verse to your friend using only the groupings of first letters to trigger your memory.

5. Quote the verse without using the sheet.

6. Repeat steps three through five as often as necessary until the verse is fixed in your mind.

Another method is to have a friend read a section to you phrase by phrase and allow you to repeat each phrase from memory.

If the one reading the verse to you can add the right voice inflections and help you visualize the words, you should be able to memorize at least three verses within ten minutes.

As you memorize, think of questions that will prompt the next part of the verse. These questions should help you establish the logic of the verse in your mind.

Once the passage is initially memorized, the following steps can be taken for meditation.

1 MAKE A COPY OF THE PASSAGE.

Just as kings were instructed in Deuteronomy 17:18 to make a personal copy of the Scriptures, so it is wise for you to have a personal copy of the passage that you are memorizing. The exercise of writing out the verses will help you to form them in your own mind. It is also helpful to separate phrases. Thus, Psalm 1:3 would read as follows:

"And he shall be like a tree

planted by the rivers of water,

that bringeth forth his fruit in his season;

his leaf also shall not wither;

and whatsoever he doeth shall prosper."

If you find it difficult to write out your own copy of the passage, make a photocopy of it or ask someone to make a copy for you.

2 PICTURE THE CONCEPT OF EACH VERSE.

The key to effective meditation is visualizing each idea in the passage. This process can begin at the very first stage of memorization. Try to draw a picture by each phrase that would illustrate or symbolize its meaning or application. The applications will multiply the more you engraft the verse into your heart.

Visualizing will require concentration, illumination by the Holy Spirit, and creativity of expression. The exercise of trying to do this will prove tremendously valuable to you in further meditation.

Psalm 1:3 could have the following pictures and associations:

The tree should look healthy. The root system should be extensive. The trunk and branches sturdy and leaves full.

Before drawing a river, we must identify whether it is a fountain, a brook, a flowing river, or an irrigation ditch.

By looking up the Hebrew word in a concordance, you will discover what the word means.

RIVER'S
it in the flags by the *r* brink	Ex 2:3	2975
walked along by the *r* side	Ex 2:5	2975
by the *r* brink against he come	Ex 7:15	2975
forth, as gardens by the *r* side	Num 24:6	5104

RIVERS
upon their streams, upon their *r*	Ex 7:19	2975
rod over the streams, over the *r*	Ex 8:5	2975
waters, in the seas, and in the *r*	Lev 11:9	5158
scales in the seas, and in the *r*	Lev 11:10	5158
to Jotbath, a land of *r* of waters	Deut 10:7	5158
r of Damascus, better than all	2Kin 5:12	5104
up all the *r* of besieged places	2Kin 19:24	2975
He shall not see the *r*, the	Job 20:17	6390
He cutteth out *r* among the rocks	Job 28:10	2975
the rock poured me out *r* of oil	Job 29:6	6388
a tree planted by the *r* of water	Ps 1:3	6388

6385. פָּלַג **pâlag**, *paw-lag'*; a prim. **root**; to *split* (lit. or fig.):—divide.

6386. פְּלַג **p°lag** (Chald.), *pel-ag'*; corresp. to 6385:—divided.

6387. פְּלַג **p°lag** (Chald.), *pel-ag'*; from 6386; a *half*:—dividing.

6388. פֶּלֶג **peleg**, *peh'-leg*; from 6385; a *rill* (i.e. small *channel* of water, as in irrigation):—river, stream.

The concept of seasonal fruit suggests care and pruning for years before fruitfulness and months between fruitful times.

Leaves that do not wither indicate surrounding barrenness in times of drought.

Christians are to bear much fruit. An overflowing bushel basket would symbolize this.

Visualization is the first exciting step in making God's Word live in our hearts. God promises that to the degree we do this we will be able to claim whatever Scripture we want to claim, and we will find that its promises will come true in our own lives.

"If ye abide in me, and my words abide in you, ye shall ask what you will, and it shall be done unto you" (John 15:7).

3 TURN THE PICTURES INTO AN ACTION SEQUENCE.

Now that you have the elements of the verse in picture form, design an action sequence in your mind as you quote the verse word for word.

"He shall be like a tree . . ."

Picture the stages of growth in a tree.

". . . Planted by the rivers of water . . ."

Irrigation requires care to bring refreshing channels of nourishment to our lives. This care can be in the form of worship services, daily Bible reading, and Godly music.

". . . Bringeth forth his fruit in his season . . ."

Bringing forth fruit involves the action of cultivating character, multiplying the seeds of spiritual life in others, and reproducing ourselves physically through marriage.

"His leaf also shall not wither . . ."

This implies that there will be drought in the surrounding area. Others will feel barrenness in their souls.

". . . And whatsoever he doeth shall prosper . . ."

The test of fruitfulness is "Does it last?" The success of our fruit will be measured in the second, third, and fourth generations of our physical and spiritual offspring.

Continue this process for Psalm 1.
Date completed _____

7 SHEEP BEGIN FEEDING IN THE MORNING.

Sheep will rise just before dawn and start to feed. By doing this they not only enjoy the cool of the day, but they also receive the special reward of dew upon the grass. Dew is actually a primary source of water for sheep. Sheep can go for months without drinking water when they take in the heavy dew of early morning grazing.

Getting up early for meditation was one of the keys to the delight that David enjoyed with the Lord and His Word.

In order for sheep to graze early in the morning, the shepherd must rise even earlier. The first activity of the shepherd in the morning is to call his sheep. Because of his consistent care and example,

they instantly recognize his voice and respond to it by following him to rich pastures.

Our Chief Shepherd illustrated this pattern as he rose when it was yet *". . . a great while before day . . ."* (Mark 1:35). He spent time alone in communion with His heavenly Father, and then He met with His disciples and "fed" them with His Word.

Two secrets to getting up early in the morning are going to bed early at night and arranging to meet somebody in the morning.

Every wise father will get up before his family in the morning and prepare himself spiritually so that he can effectively carry out a morning *Wisdom Search* from the Word with his family.

For several years one father got up in the early morning hours to memorize Scripture. During the day he would review it out loud, and at night he would quote it to his children as they went to sleep.

Today his thirteen-year-old daughter can quote the entire book of James, Romans 6 and 8, Matthew 5, 6, and 7, the book of Jude, and many Psalms.

When his ten-year-old daughter was three, she came up to him and said, "Daddy, I know 'behold.'" He said, "What do you mean?" She then quoted Psalm 134, having learned it simply by listening to her father repeating it out loud.

His seven-year-old son can quote the first ten chapters of Proverbs, Matthew 5 and 6, Romans 6, Ruth 1–2, James 1, and several other chapters.

His three-year-old son is able to recite Matthew 5 as well as the Greek and English alphabet and several Greek words.

The radiance of this family is a striking testimony to the power of the Word of God. The day after Christmas a fire broke out in their home, and they lost all of their earthly possessions. As neighbors responded in meeting their needs and saw their peace and contentment and joy in the Lord, some wept, and they listened in awe as the children quoted Scriptures which were now more valuable to this family than anything they had lost in the fire.

This father uses curiosity to help him memorize Scripture. He covers the words of the passage except for the phrase that he is working on. After visualizing that phrase, he will wonder what the next phrase says. He continues this process until the entire chapter is visualized and memorized.

This family is enrolled in the Advanced Training Institute of America, and the skills that they have developed in memorizing Scripture have carried over into all academic disciplines.

If I were to get up two hours before I had to go to work, I would rise at _____. In order to get sufficient sleep, I would have to go to bed at _____. Date I began doing this _____.

8 SHEEP MUST BE AT REST BEFORE THEY CAN CHEW THEIR FOOD.

Distractions and irritations will stop sheep from ruminating on their food. One source of irritation is insects which are naturally attracted to sheep. Insects are especially bothersome to the head and face of sheep.

In order to free his sheep from this damaging distraction, the shepherd will pour a specially prepared oil mixture over the head of the sheep. This mixture contains oil, tar, and herbs. The tar repels insects, while the oil and herbs bring healing to the sheep when they have been scratched by thorns or bitten by insects.

There is nothing more damaging or disruptive to the process of meditation than worldly cares and irritating distractions. Our Chief Shepherd has given to us the Holy Spirit, Who instructs us not to worry over anything, but to tell God every detail of our needs in earnest and thankful prayer. The peace of God, which transcends human understanding, will then keep guard over our hearts and minds as we rest in Christ Jesus. (See Philippians 4:6–7.)

PREPARATIONS FOR QUIETNESS

During the day, get alone in a "prayer closet." By shutting out the distractions of the world, we can bring up the Word which we have read, studied, and memorized, and use it for prayer, intercession, supplication, and thanksgiving before the Lord. God has promised that those who do this secretly will be rewarded openly.

Daniel had major responsibilities as the leading president of a world empire. Yet, three times a day he resorted to his "prayer closet" and worshiped the Lord.

The resulting success in Daniel's life and ministry is a living testimony of the importance of following his example.

Bible Art Series, Standard Publishing, Cincinnati
Daniel

Further instructions for meditation are contained in Deuteronomy 6:7. "... *Talk of them when thou sittest in thine house, and when thou walkest by the way, and when thou liest down, and when thou risest up.*"

... As you relax.   ... As you go to work.

... As you sleep.   ... As you wake up.

Perhaps the most important of these four occasions occurs while we are going to sleep at night. This observation is based upon the fact that God designed the day to begin in the evening. "... *The evening and the morning were the first day*" *(Genesis 1:5).*

Furthermore, the last thoughts on our minds before we go to sleep will be on our subconscious mind throughout the night and will set our mental attitude for the next day, either consciously or unconsciously.

It is for this reason that God gives special commands to meditate on His Word during this time. "*Stand in awe, and sin not: commune with your own heart upon your bed, and be still ...*" *(Psalm 4:4).*

One of David's responses to this command is found in Psalm 63:5–6. *"My soul shall be satisfied as with marrow and fatness; and my mouth shall praise thee with joyful lips: When I remember thee upon my bed, and meditate on thee in the night watches."*

An eighty-five year old Christian widow would often wake up in the middle of the night with fears; then she would spend her days in loneliness and depression. One day a family visited her and challenged her to begin memorizing Scripture. Soon she could quote the book of James, the Gospel of John, all of Titus, and several chapters of Revelation. Her depression left, her loneliness was overcome, and she stated, "Whenever I wake up at night, I just meditate on Scripture, and I fall right back to sleep."

9 SHEEP REFINE THEIR FOOD DURING THE FIRST "CHEWING."

Often while grazing, sheep will swallow sticks and stones along with the grass and plants. These larger objects go into the first compartment of the stomach, the *rumen*. These undigestible items are not allowed to pass through the digestive system but are brought up again during rumination so that they can be expelled.

In our studies of Scripture it is easy to add human presuppositions and inaccurate connotations to what God's Word is really saying. Therefore, the vital first step in meditation is to bring each thought that we have under the scrutiny of the principles of Scripture and to throw out those ideas which are not consistent with it.

"(For the weapons of our warfare are not carnal, but mighty through God to the pulling down of strong holds;) Casting down imaginations, and every high thing that exalteth itself against the knowledge of God, and bringing into captivity every thought to the obedience of Christ" (II Corinthians 10:4–5).

Once the undigestible food is removed from the rumen, the remaining food is passed into the second stomach compartment, called the *reticulum*. Here, the food is turned into soft clumps which are called *cuds*.

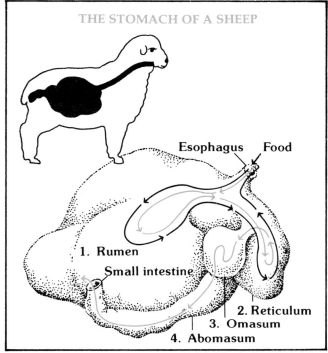

From *World Book Encyclopedia*©1985 World Book

10 SHEEP GAIN MAXIMUM BENEFIT FROM THEIR FOOD AS THEY RECHEW IT.

Digestive juices are found only in the fourth compartment of the digestive tract. The processes which occur between the first and the fourth compartments contain significant analogies to the steps of meditation on Scripture.

The grass and plants which sheep eat contain *cellulose* (a wood product from which the pages of our Bibles are made). Sheep cannot digest cellulose. During the rumination process, sheep grind up the cuds to a very fine pulp. This grinding usually takes two "chewings," after which the food goes to the third stomach compartment called the *omasum* (ō-**mā**-səm).

The bacteria and protozoa within the sheep's omasum are able to break down the cellulose. The pulp then passes into the fourth compartment of the stomach called the *abomasum* (ab-ō-**mā**-səm). Here the digestive juices begin to act upon the cud. In the process, they digest the bacteria and protozoa. Thus, sheep get nourishment from meat while ruminating on the grass.

15

Similarly, the Holy Spirit transforms Scripture into spiritual "meat" through the process of meditation.

Liquids which the sheep drink do not go through the rumination process. In the same way, Christians who are immature in the faith are nourished by the "milk of the Word." This "nourishment" could be compared to simply reading or hearing Scripture.

"For every one that useth milk is unskilful in the word of righteousness: for he is a babe. But strong meat belongeth to them that are of full age, even those who by reason of use have their senses exercised to discern both good and evil" (Hebrews 5:13–14).

HOW DOES MEMORIZATION DIFFER FROM REVIEW?

Many who have memorized Scripture have become discouraged because they soon forget what they have memorized. This concern is needless and shows lack of understanding of the true nature of meditation.

The purpose of memorization is not to see how many chapters we can quote, but rather to prepare us for the daily process of meditation. This process is of paramount importance to God.

The principles of this process are clearly pictured in God's provision of manna: It had to be gathered each day. Yesterday's manna became stale, a fact which forced the people to depend upon the Lord daily and to live in proper reverence of Him.

There is need to review Scriptures so we can have material upon which to meditate and with which to worship the Lord in Spirit and in truth; *"... for the Father seeketh such to worship him" (John 4:23).*

Simply reviewing chapters may appeal to the sense of accomplishment of our soul and can lead to pride. Actually, there is no loss in forgetting what we have memorized, since there is great value in rememorizing it and seeing new insights from it.

There is benefit, however, in memorizing as much as possible. The conscious mind may forget a passage; however, the Spirit will bring it to our attention whenever it is needed. Memorized Scripture is like the snow bank described in Isaiah 55:10–11.

"For as the rain cometh down, and the snow from heaven, and returneth not thither, but watereth the earth, and maketh it bring forth and bud, that it may give seed to the sower, and bread to the eater: So shall my word be that goeth forth out of my mouth: it shall not return unto me void, but it shall accomplish that which I please, and it shall prosper in the thing whereto I sent it."

Just as snow comes into a cold atmosphere, we may memorize God's Word with a cold heart and even forget what we have memorized; however, the snow does not go away, and when God warms up our hearts, the Word "melts" into our consciousness and accomplishes its purposes.

HOW DOES MEMORIZATION DIFFER FROM MEDITATION?

Once the steps of memorization have taken place, meditation can begin. In memorization we confirm the interpretation of a passage; in meditation we discover its applications to our lives. There is only one interpretation of Scripture. (See II Peter 1:20.) However, there are an infinite number of applications.

The Holy Spirit guides us to the right interpretation of Scripture as we study the context, the original languages, the historical setting, and the sentence structure of a passage. We are led to correct applications as the Holy Spirit takes the Word and directs it to specific needs and situations.

Each application must be in full harmony with the interpretation and must not be contrary to any other Scripture. Paul based sound teaching on Christ's own words and on that which leads to Christlike living. (See I Timothy 6:3.)

Paul's teaching is also consistent with the emphasis of Joshua 1:8, *"... that thou mayest observe to do according to all that is written therein. ..."*

Jesus confirmed the need to study the whole Bible when He taught, *"... Man shall not live by bread alone, but by every word that proceedeth out of the mouth of God" (Matthew 4:4).*

Two other factors must be considered if we are to glean accurate application from meditation: the cleansing of guilt and the removal of bitterness. These two poisons of the soul and spirit will corrupt the Word and cause us to misapply it in daily situations.

Great damage is done when Scripture is inaccurately applied. For this reason, we must know the Scriptures, memorizing as much as possible so that when we meditate on them day and night, we can compare spiritual concepts with spiritual realities and enjoy the rewards of spiritual discernment.

HOW MEDITATION TAKES PLACE

DEFINITIONS OF MEDITATION

- Meditation is a pleasant "murmuring" of Scripture to yourself.
  *". . . In his law doth he **meditate** . . ." (Psalm 1:2).*
  Hagah: to murmur (in pleasure); to ponder.

- Meditation is a quiet reflection upon the words of Scripture.
  *". . . Thy testimonies are my **meditation**" (Psalm 119:99).*
  Siychah: reflection with deep devotion; contemplation; thoughtful utterances of Scripture.

- Meditation is a musical repetition of God's Word.
  *"Let the words of my mouth, and the **meditation** of my heart . . ." (Psalm 19:14).*
  Higgayown: a musical notation; a murmuring sound.

- Meditation is a prayerful reviewing of Scripture.
  *"**Meditate** upon these things . . ." (I Timothy 4:15).*
  Meletao: to carefully revolve in the mind; to muse upon.

- Meditation is a communing with God in the language of His own written Word.
  *"My hands also will I lift up unto thy commandments, which I have loved; and I will **meditate** in thy statutes" (Psalm 119:48).*
  Meditation is "talking to the King in the King's own words."

- Meditation is building your day and night around Scripture.

*"O how love I thy law! it is my **meditation** all the day" (Psalm 119:97).*
". . . I have esteemed the words of his mouth more than my necessary food" (Job 23:12).

- Meditation is that sweet fellowship that comes from worshiping God in spirit and in truth.
  *"My **meditation** of him shall be sweet . . ." (Psalm 104:34).*

Christians can follow these four steps to fulfill these aspects of meditation:

1. PRAYING THE PASSAGE BACK TO GOD.

God delights in hearing His Word. He has magnified it above all His name. (See Psalm 138:2.) When we take a passage of Scripture that we have memorized and use it to commune with the Lord, we are thinking God's thoughts after Him. We are talking to the King in the King's own language.

Thus, to meditate on Psalm 1 would be to say "O Lord, blessed is the man that walketh not in the counsel of the ungodly, nor standeth in the way of sinners, nor sitteth in the seat of the scornful, but his delight is in [Thy law O Lord]; and in [Thy] law doth he meditate day and night. He shall be like a tree. . . ."

2. REPEAT EACH WORD WITH EMPHASIS.

Meditation is going over the same Scripture, but each time with different emphasis. Therefore, the following emphasis and understanding could be given to the passage.

*". . . **He** shall be like a tree . . ."*
*". . . He **shall** be like a tree . . ."*
*". . . He shall **be** like a tree . . ."*
*". . . He shall be **like** a tree . . ."*
*". . . He shall be like **a** tree . . ."*
*". . . He shall be like a **tree** . . ."*

After repeating each phrase, visualize how that truth could apply to your life asking the Lord for special insight and understanding. The insights may not come immediately; they may even come the next day as the Word speaks to you in the way. Nevertheless, God will answer your prayer.

3. PERSONALIZE THE PASSAGE.

With an understanding of what the passage is actually saying, we can now put it in the first person and make it our own.

[I] shall be like a tree . . . planted by the rivers of water, that bringeth forth [my] fruit in [my] season; [my] leaf also shall not wither; and whatsoever [I do] shall prosper.

4. VISUALIZE APPLICATIONS FROM EACH WORD.

The richness of Scripture meditation can only be hinted at in these few lines. However, they may serve to indicate the inexhaustibility of Scriptural application.

". . . He shall be like a tree . . ."

What kind of a "tree" am I now—a wild apple, a weeping willow, or a mighty oak?
Is my core hard wood or soft wood?
Have storms strengthened or weakened me?

". . . Planted by the rivers of water . . ."

How and when was I planted [new birth]?
Can people tell how "old" I am spiritually?
Who are the ones who have nurtured me?
What are my irrigation channels?
Have I taken in the nourishment of the Word?
Do I worship regularly in church?
Do I strengthen my spirit with singing?

". . . That bringeth forth his fruit in his season . . ."

What is spiritual fruit?
What fruit does God expect from me?
What are my seasons of fruitbearing?
How much fruit have I already borne?
Is pruning needed if I am to bear more fruit?
What kind of pruning would God do in my life?

As you ask and answer questions like these, the Holy Spirit will draw upon related passages and will produce exciting dimensions of spiritual understanding and growth. *"When thou goest, it shall lead thee; when thou sleepest, it shall keep thee; and when thou awakest, it shall talk with thee" (Proverbs 6:22).*

11 SHEEP MUST HAVE A BALANCE BETWEEN EATING AND EXERCISE.

If sheep spend too much time eating and ruminating, they will build up layers of fat. Obesity is a dangerous condition, since it is then easy for the sheep to roll over during a time of rumination. Rolling over is called *casting*.

When a sheep is in this condition its center of gravity shifts so that it cannot right itself. Stomach gasses begin to swell the sheep's stomach. The bloated stomach cuts off circulation to the feet, and the sheep is no longer able to stand upon them. The ultimate consequence of casting is death.

God has placed significant warnings in Scripture for us to maintain a balance between the study of the Word and its application. The imbalance caused by study without application is strongly condemned in James 1:

> *"But be ye doers of the word, and not hearers only, deceiving your own selves.*
>
> *"For if any be a hearer of the word, and not a doer, he is like unto a man beholding his natural face in a glass:*
>
> *"For he beholdeth himself, and goeth his way, and straightway forgetteth what manner of man he was.*
>
> *"But whoso looketh into the perfect law of liberty, and continueth therein, he being not a forgetful hearer, but a doer of the work, this man shall be blessed in his deed"* (James 1:22–25).

Many pastors of local churches have affirmed that the two groups of members who cause the most trouble are those who get too little spiritual food and those who get "too much" spiritual food (knowledge without application).

12 SHEEP WHICH WANDER CAN "MUNCH" THEIR WAY INTO SERIOUS DANGER.

Sheep that become independent soon stray away from the safety of the shepherd and the flock. They are actually drawn away by their own appetites as they go from one clump of grass to another. Thus, they expose themselves to a multitude of dangers.

The sheep's thick coat of wool can easily be caught in the underbrush of thickets, causing the sheep to be held captive until it dies.

A lone sheep is also an open invitation to one of its many predators. Without the protection of the shepherd, a wolf, a lion, or a bear would quickly kill and devour the sheep.

Further dangers for sheep involve falling into crevices, picking up parasites, eating poisonous plants, or casting. A wise shepherd is aware of all of these dangers. Therefore, if he sees that one of his sheep is persistent in going its own way, he will resort to administering the pain of discipline. He will lovingly break one of its legs and then nurse the sheep back to health.

This close association between shepherd and sheep establishes a special bond which continues after the leg is healed. It was this picture that David had in mind when he wrote the words, *"Make me to hear joy and gladness; that the bones which thou hast broken may rejoice"* (Psalm 51:8).

It is during times of such discipline that meditation becomes especially cherished and valuable to the Christian.

"I have gone astray like a lost sheep; seek thy servant; for I do not forget thy commandments" (Psalm 119:176).

REPORTS OF TRUE SUCCESS

HOW MEDITATION OVERCAME LEARNING DISABILITIES

"While in grade school, I was labeled an "LD" (learning disability) child. Then last summer my parents, who are both Seminar alumni, encouraged me to attend the Basic Seminar. At the end of the week I immediately started memorizing Romans 6. When I went back to school in the fall, instead of struggling and just making average grades, I made the honor roll! Praise God, it really works."

A seventeen-year-old girl from Pennsylvania

HOW A MEDICAL STUDENT EXCELLED THROUGH MEDITATION

"I was a third year medical student when I attended the Basic Youth Conflicts Seminar. Because I felt like I had no defenses against Satan, I vowed to memorize Scripture five minutes a day. As time went on, I found myself spending more and more time memorizing Scripture. Soon it became one hour a day, and two hours on Sunday and Wednesday. All this time my grades at med school have steadily gone up, despite tougher competition. I am now in the 99th percentile nationally. I praise God, not so much for good grades, but for His Word that has the power to change lives."

A second-year resident doctor from Illinois

HOW MEDITATION WORKED FOR ONE WHO DID NOT THINK IT WOULD WORK

"The principle of success made me dizzy when I attended my second Seminar. I knew in my heart that the success stories must be true, but I didn't think that they would work for me. However, I promised God that I would try meditation because I was really having trouble at school. I memorized and meditated every night for the rest of the summer. When report cards came out I had an 'A' in English, as well as an 'A' in my other weak subject, algebra."

A fourteen-year-old boy from Texas

HOW MEDITATION IS GREATER THAN THE POWER OF ANY SIN

"I praise God for the unfathomable riches of His Word. Five years ago I was at the very top of your reprobation chart. But now after three Seminars and a continuous program of meditation on Scripture, I am living proof that it does work. God is restoring the years that the locusts have eaten, and He continues to open my eyes to more of Himself."

An alumnus from Georgia

HOW THE "HIDDEN WORD" DISPLACED A HIDDEN HEART

"When I was eleven years old, I was confronted with a situation of immorality for which I was totally unprepared. At that time I was unsaved, and I responded wrongly with the result that ever since that time, a deep-seated, wrong outlook has twisted my view of life. The Lord directed my attention to the moral freedom section of the Seminar. I reexamined the cycles of life. This concept, coupled with engrafting Romans 6 and the principles of identification in *The Eagle Story*, has enabled me to gain victory in an area that was buried for twenty-nine years. I am now enjoying a tremendous new freedom with the Lord and in my contact with people."

A businessman from California

HOW TO GET STARTED

- Determine the person to whom you will be accountable for memorization and meditation (your father, husband, pastor, or friend).
- Ask this person to select a passage of Scripture and set a date for completion. (See pages 4–5.)
- Schedule a time to quote the Scripture.
- Work with your pastor to organize an elective accountability class at church during which memorized Scripture could be quoted and important insights shared. This class could include all age levels.